RHINO COMES TO AMERICA,
A.
Maynard

A RHINO
COMES TO AMERICA

★  ★

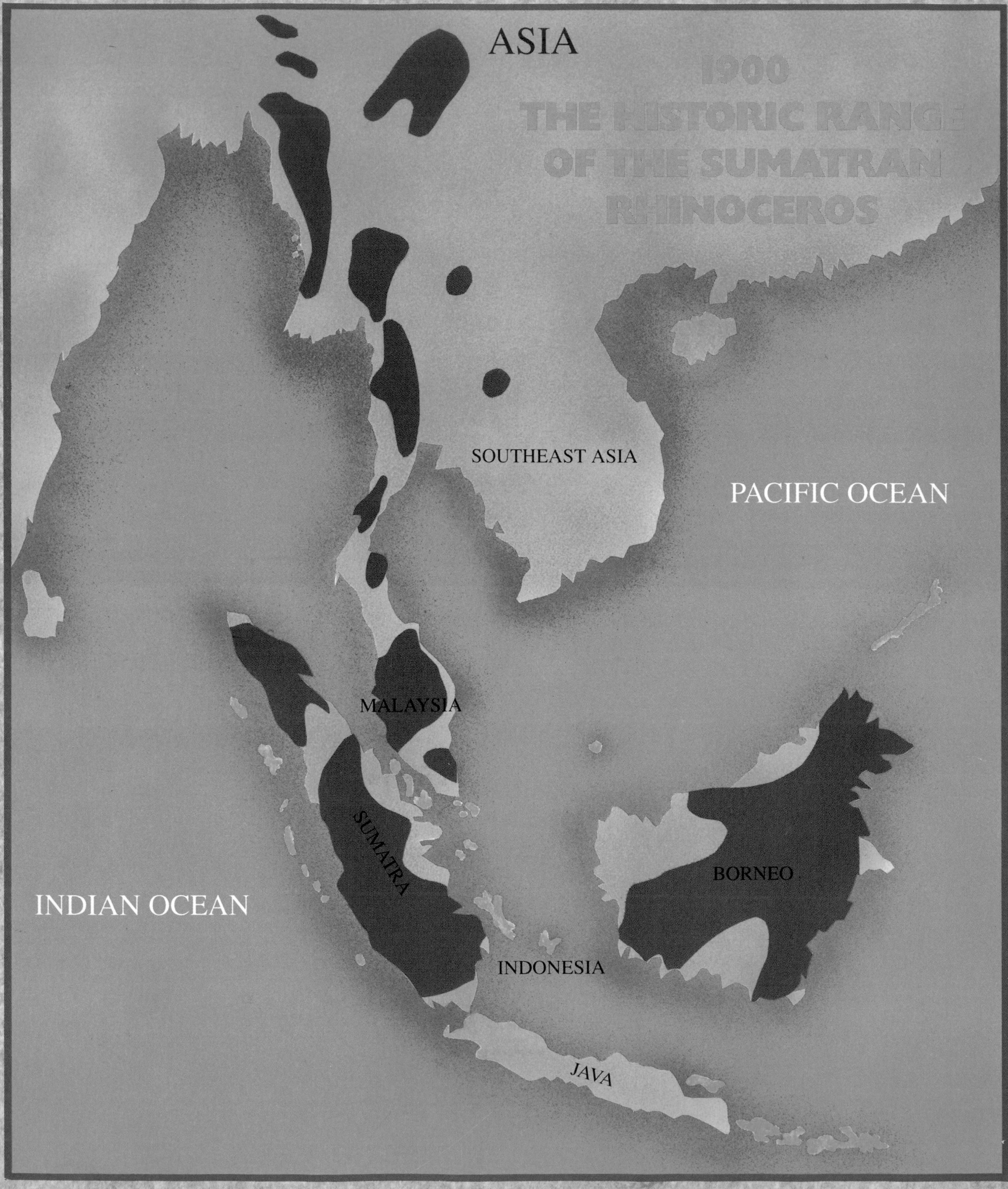

ASIA
1900
THE HISTORIC RANGE
OF THE SUMATRAN
RHINOCEROS
SOUTHEAST ASIA
PACIFIC OCEAN
MALAYSIA
SUMATRA
BORNEO
INDIAN OCEAN
INDONESIA
JAVA

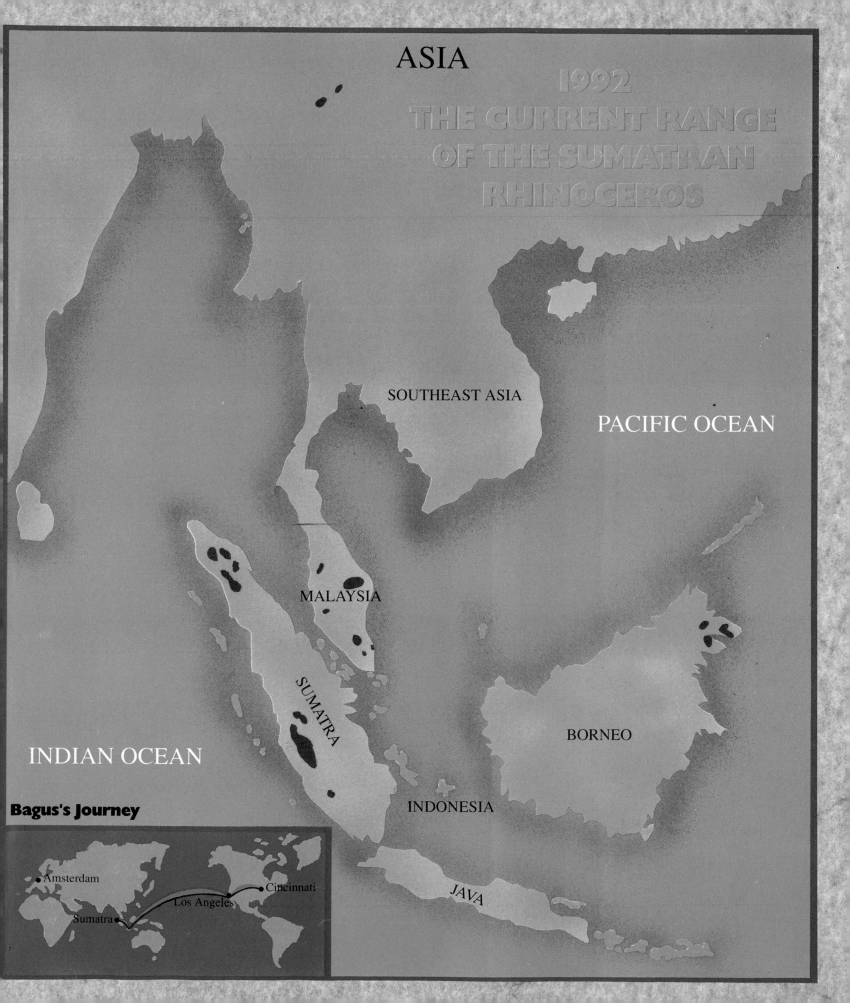

ASIA

1992
THE CURRENT RANGE
OF THE SUMATRAN
RHINOCEROS

SOUTHEAST ASIA

PACIFIC OCEAN

MALAYSIA

SUMATRA

INDIAN OCEAN

BORNEO

INDONESIA

JAVA

Bagus's Journey

Amsterdam

Cincinnati

Los Angeles

Sumatra

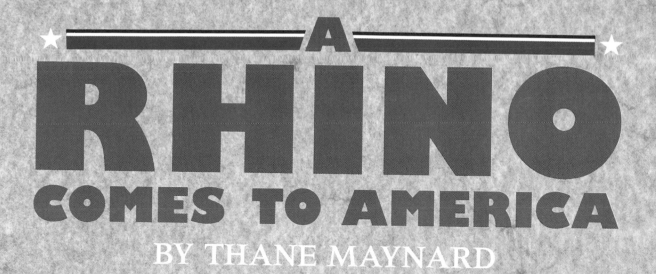

A RHINO
COMES TO AMERICA

BY THANE MAYNARD

A Cincinnati Zoo Book

FRANKLIN WATTS
New York ■ Chicago ■ London ■ Toronto ■ Sydney

This book is dedicated to the man who
got me into the field of wildlife conservation,
Dr. EDWARD MARUSKA,
leader of the Cincinnati Zoo
for more than thirty years.

Photographs copyright ©: Ron Austing: frontis, pp. 3, 5, 6, 28, 29, 31, 33, 36; Mike Delaney: 7 top left; Stan Rullman: pp. 14, 15, 16, 34, 35; Los Angeles Zoo: pp. 7 center right, 12 top, 19; all other photographs copyright © Cincinnati Zoo.

Library of Congress Cataloging-in-Publication Data

Maynard, Thane.
A rhino comes to America / by Thane Maynard.
p.   cm. — (A Cincinnati Zoo book)
Includes bibliographical references (p.   ) and index.
Summary: Describes the status of the Sumatran rhinoceros as one of the most endangered animals in the world and relates the story of Bagus, a specimen who was captured in the wild and sent to the Cincinnati Zoo as part of a new breeding program to save the species from extinction.
ISBN 0-531-11173-3 (lib. bdg.). — ISBN 0-531-15258-8 (trade)
1. Bagus (Rhinoceros)—Juvenile literature.   2. Sumatran rhinoceros—Ohio—Cincinnati—Biography—Juvenile literature.
3. Sumatran rhinoceros—Juvenile literature.   [1. Bagus (Rhinoceros) 2. Sumatran rhinoceros. 3. Rhinoceroses. 4. Rare animals. 5. Wildlife conservation.] I. Title. II. Series.
QL737.U63M415   1993
636'.9728—dc20
92-27283 CIP AC

In Sumatra, where Bagus was born, the word *bagus* means "Great!" You might answer *"Bagus,"* when a friend asks how you are doing. This (above) is Bagus's forest home, but as people move into the area, the trees are cut, leaving less space for the rhinos.

BAGUS

BAGUS (pronounced "bag-goose") is a 950-pound (431-kg) rhinoceros who was born in a tropical forest in northern Sumatra, the westernmost island in the nation of Indonesia. Today, Bagus lives at the Cincinnati Zoo and Botanical Garden, in Cincinnati, Ohio. You might be wondering what a Sumatran rhino is doing in the middle of a big American city. The answer is that being there is saving his life and helping save his *species*.

Bagus is one of the last of his kind, for Sumatran rhinos are one of the most *endangered* animals in the world. One problem these mammals face is that people are *poaching* rhinos for their horns, but their biggest problem is *deforestation*, the destruction of their home in the wild. More and more people are crowding into the islands where the rhinos live, which means less and less space is left for the rhinos. As a result, there may be fewer than eight hundred Sumatran rhinos alive today.

This is Bagus's story

RHINO LIFE IN THE WILD

The first time you see a Sumatran rhinoceros you are pretty sure it's a rhino. After all, it is a big, wide-bodied, hoofed animal with two small horns sticking up over its nose. But it doesn't look much like the larger and more famous rhinos from Africa and India that you're used to seeing in zoos.

Bagus's two small horns are not made of bone, as are most animals' horns. They are tightly packed masses of fibers, like matted hair.

The first difference you might notice is that Sumatran rhinos, unlike other rhinos, have hair growing over most of their bodies, leading to their other name, "the hairy rhino."

Sumatran rhinos are the most primitive of the five species, or kinds, of rhinoceros alive today, which means scientists think they are the most like the ancient rhinos that lived on Earth thirty million years ago.

They stand 4 to 4½ feet (1.2 m to 1.4 m) tall at the shoulder and weigh between 1,000 and 2,000 pounds (454 and 907 kg) when they are fully grown, which makes them the smallest of all five species of rhino. The white rhinoceros from southern Africa can weigh over 6,000 pounds (2,722 kg).

The five species (clockwise from top left): black rhino and white (tan in color) rhino of Africa; and Indian, Sumatran, and Javan rhinos of Asia.

One reason for the size difference may be the *habitat* where they live. The black rhinoceros and the white rhinoceros of Africa live in the open grasslands, or savannahs, while Sumatran rhinos come from the dense rain forests of Indonesia and Malaysia. Their smaller size makes it easier for them to move through the forest, which provides them with plenty of places to hide.

The dense forest also makes it difficult for scientists to observe this species in the wild. In the rain forests where they live, the thick growth of plants on the forest floor makes it difficult to even find a rhino. In addition, the animals are extremely elusive, and roam over a wide *range*, often walking many miles at a time. So most of the research on the Sumatran rhino is through indirect observation. Scientists study their tracks (footprints), their droppings, and other marks they leave behind, such as signs of feeding, foot scrapings in the soil, and urine scent. To keep track of individual rhinos, researchers make plaster casts of their tracks and study them very carefully until they can tell one animal from another.

In the thick tropical forest, a rhino can seem almost invisible.

Every trace the elusive rhinos leave behind is studied.
Above: Like a human's fingerprint, this plaster cast of a rhino's
10-inch (25-cm)-long hoofprint can be used to identify the animal.
Below: A scientist tests the depth of a rhino wallow.

A newborn Sumatran rhino (above) and a six-month-old calf (right), in the zoo in Jakarta, Indonesia

Most of the year, Sumatran rhinos live alone in the forest, but the males and females come together for brief mating periods. Sumatran rhinos are pregnant for about fifteen months, after which a single 70- to 80-pound (32- to 36-kg) baby is born. The two parent rhinos then stay together while the female nurses the calf. This lasts for about fourteen to eighteen months, while the calf grows very quickly to about three-quarters of its adult size. The rhino will not bear another calf for three or four years.

The rhinos follow well-established trails through the forest. The vegetation along these game trails is worn down, for they are also used by other forest dwellers including tapirs, tigers, and leopards. Male Sumatran rhinos travel over a larger range than do females, and often cover several miles between feeding stops. Both sexes visit natural salt licks (which provide additional minerals) at regular intervals. Pregnant female rhinos and those nursing a calf have been seen leaving their home range higher on the slopes to be closer to a salt lick.

Sumatran rhinos are browsers, feeding almost entirely on leaves and new shoots from saplings, trees, and some undergrowth plants. At times they even bend or break small trees to reach the leaves. They eat fallen fruits, too, and a wide variety of plant species. They don't eat a great deal at one time, but sample new leaves in one area and then move to another, often a long distance away. Field researchers have seen them feed on over 150 different plant species.

Water, dust, or mud holes are all good places for rhino wallows.

Sumatran rhinos spend most of the night feeding and much of the day wallowing in mud holes. Several times a day they cover their bodies with mud. This may keep the skin moist and protect the animals from biting and stinging insects. If their skin becomes too dry, it may crack and become infected. Wild boar, deer, and even elephants use the mud holes, too, but the rhinos use them more regularly.

RHINOS IN DANGER

Even though tigers, the largest cats in the world, live in the same rain forests, the only *predators* that really threaten Sumatran rhinos are people. Humans have hunted all species of rhinoceros for centuries, but the development of the rifle has made it easier for hunters and harder for the rhinos in the last two hundred years. All five rhino species are endangered, and today it is illegal to kill rhinos. With this protection, they are no longer killed for food or sport. However, some people believe that a rhino's horns have medicinal value, and they will pay thousands of dollars for them. People pay just with money, but the rhinos pay with their lives.

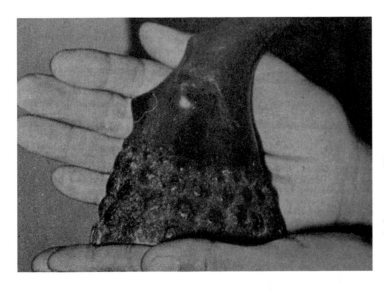

Poachers are still killing rhinos. A horn like this one, shown in a newspaper photo, can be sold for a large sum.

A bigger problem for the Sumatran rhinoceros is *habitat destruction*. The rhinos cannot find the plants they need for food and cover in a bean field or on a palm tree plantation. They need the plant life found in the rain forest. But every year thousands of acres of their habitat are cleared for farms or logging. The rhinos are then forced into smaller and smaller ranges. Unfortunately, this makes it easier for poachers to find them. So, except in a few national parks in Indonesia where they receive some protection, Sumatran rhinos are rapidly vanishing from the wild.

The Sumatran rhinoceros lives in places other than the island of Sumatra. At one time it ranged throughout much of Southeast Asia. However, it now inhabits only isolated pockets of the tropical forests of Thailand, Malaysia, Borneo, and Sumatra. The rhino's name comes from the fact that the largest *population* lives in Sumatra.

Rhino habitat disappears as the jungle is cleared for rice paddies (right) or rubber plantations (above).

In Mt. Leuser National Park rhinos have a safe place to live.

RHINO RESCUE

Human encroachment and illegal poaching are hurting the Sumatran rhinoceros. Conservation organizations list the rhino as one of the twelve most threatened animals on Earth. Today, fortunately, people are working to save this beautiful species by protecting the rhinos most in danger of being killed and by trying to increase the rhino population through *captive breeding*.

Wildlife refuges and national parks have been established to give rhinos and other animals safe areas in which to live. Most of the eight hundred Sumatran rhinos that are left on Earth now live in protected areas. About two hundred live in Mt. Leuser National Park, in northern Sumatra. In the central region of the island, Kerinci-Seblat National Park, one of the largest reserves in Indonesia, provides 5,790 square miles (15,000 sq km) of forest habitat for up to half of all the Sumatran rhinos living today. These areas are closely guarded against poachers, and the rhinos are given protection not available outside the parks.

Another part of the effort to save the rhinos involves capturing some animals and moving them from unprotected areas in the wild to breeding facilities in captivity. These special breeding facilities keep the threatened species safe from extinction while protected areas are established. Only species that are considered doomed—have no chance of survival in the wild because of human encroachment—are a part of this conservation strategy. Bagus is an example of an animal that needs this kind of rescue effort. The forests where he once lived have been cleared for the development of oil-palm plantations, and rhinos cannot survive there. Through captive breeding, it is hoped that the number of Sumatran rhinos will increase.

Black rhinos at a captive-breeding center

To help the Sumatran rhino, four North American zoos—the Cincinnati Zoo, the San Diego Zoo, the Los Angeles Zoo, and New York's Bronx Zoo—established the Sumatran Rhino Trust to work together in a captive-breeding program. In 1987 the Trust signed a cooperative agreement with the government of Indonesia. Rhinos would be captured in the wild. Some would stay in Indonesia for a breeding program in the species' native country. Others would be sent to the American zoos for their breeding programs.

Rhino experts from Indonesia, Europe, and the United States set out to capture Sumatran rhinos for the Sumatran Rhino Trust. The first four rhinos captured were females. One was named Mahatu and was transported to the Cincinnati Zoo in 1988, to become the first Sumatran rhino exhibited in the United States since 1902. It took two more years before a male rhino was caught, and that one stayed in the Indonesian facility. Finally, late in 1990, Bagus was captured in the forest near Bengkulu in Sumatra and began a long journey to America to become the first male rhino in this new captive-breeding program.

Captive-breeding programs can help save rhinos. This three-month-old Indian rhino calf, seen with the mother rhino, was born at the Los Angeles Zoo.

TO CATCH A RHINO

Sumatran rhinos may not be the biggest rhinos in the world, but they may be the hardest to catch. Since they live in thick tropical forests, they can't be spotted from miles away and chased down by truck. Instead, scientists from the capture team had to make traps in the forest on the rhino paths, hoping that the rhinos would fall into them.

TRAPPING BAGUS
(Above) Workers dug a pit and lined the pit (facing page, top) with wood planks and leaves. (Bottom, left) They covered the pit with branches and earth, and waited for a rhino to come along (bottom, right) and fall in.

The best rhino trap is a rectangular pit dug in the ground and covered by a trapdoor, soil, and leaves. The pits aren't deep enough for rhinos to get hurt, just deep enough so that they can't get out. Leaves are piled over the floor of the pit to soften the animals' fall. Fortunately for the pit diggers, rhinos aren't good climbers, so the holes don't have to be more than 4 feet (1.2 m) deep.

Still, it is not as easy as it sounds. Even though scientists study the behavior and movements of Sumatran rhinos in the forest, they can't just go out and catch one. Because these animals are so rare and shy, it took many months to catch the first rhino. Once one is captured, workers dig out one end of the pit to make a ramp, and the rhino is led up into a temporary pen.

Bagus, in a crate, was transported through the forest.
The crate was rolled over logs to the river's edge,
then floated across the river on a raft.
On the other side of the river, Bagus's crate was
loaded onto a truck and driven to Bengkulu.

FLYING RHINO

Bagus began his 9,000-mile (14,481-km) trip to Cincinnati in the winter of 1990. First he stayed for a few months in the special breeding facility in Sumatra where he learned to eat hay and grain, because they would be important parts of his zoo diet. Eventually, he was loaded in a gigantic wooden crate that weighed more than a ton once Bagus was in it. Many people had to push the crate up a ramp onto a big truck. The truck was driven to the airport in Jakarta, Indonesia, where Bagus was loaded into the cargo bay of a KLM cargo jet plane and flown to Los Angeles, California. Bagus was not drugged or "knocked out" during his travels. This would have made the trip much more dangerous for him. If he were drugged, his health and condition could

At Bengkulu, workers built a temporary pen for Bagus.

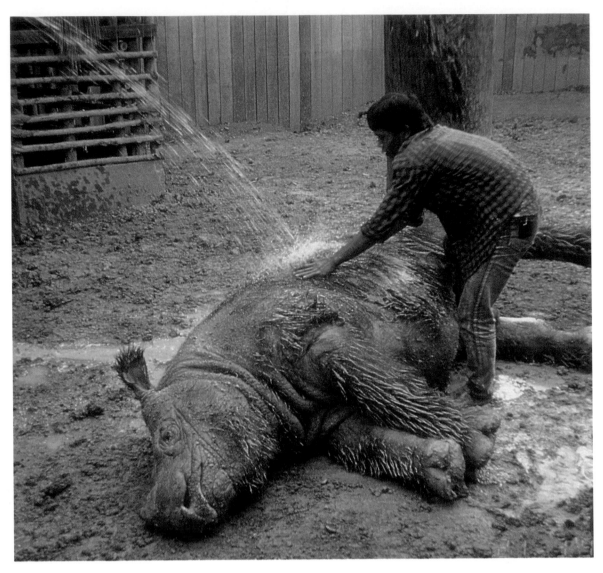

Living in captivity meant that Bagus had to get used to a new diet, and to people. Here one of the animal keepers in Indonesia hoses down Bagus.

not have been monitored along the way. Instead, special permission was given for a zoo veterinarian and a zoo keeper, Steve Romo, who is in charge of all the hoofed animals at the Cincinnati Zoo, to travel with him in the plane. During the flight Bagus rested fairly calmly, sometimes feeding on the leaves and hay in his crate. After refueling in Amsterdam, the plane flew to Los Angeles. From there, Bagus was taken by truck to the San Diego, California, zoo.

PIT STOP

Winter is a very hard time to move from the steaming hot jungle of Sumatra to the midwestern United States where the temperature often goes below 0 degrees Fahrenheit (−18 degrees Celsius) in January and February. So, Bagus stayed at the San Diego Zoo for a seven-month stopover on his way to the Cincinnati Zoo.

Climate wasn't the only reason San Diego was chosen for this winter pit stop. This zoo was home to a female Sumatran rhino, and scientists hoped that while Bagus was in California he might mate with Barakas, the zoo's adult female who had been brought to the United States three years before. Unfortunately, Barakas was more interested in Bagus than he was in her, and the two never mated successfully.

Bagus with Barakas nudging him to get up, at the San Diego Zoo

In the fall of 1991, Bagus was flown east from San Diego to the Cincinnati Zoo, where the new Sumatran rhino exhibit was ready for his arrival. A special cargo plane that could hold the huge crate flew nonstop to Ypsilanti, Michigan, 225 miles (362 km) from Cincinnati. Bagus's new keepers met him there with an animal truck and drove him to his new home.

HOME IN CINCINNATI
Before Bagus arrived from Indonesia, the outdoor rhino yard at the Cincinnati Zoo had been used only by Mahatu, the female Sumatran rhino who was to be his mate. The keepers gave the two animals a chance to get used to each other through a few

Mahatu, a female Sumatran rhino

weeks of living in the same general area before being put together. Zoo workers were eager to see how Bagus would behave when first introduced to Mahatu. The rhinos could see and smell each other from their separate enclosures, but they had never been in the same yard. When the two rhinos were finally let out in the yard together, there was a lot of snorting, wailing, and pushing before they settled down and tolerated one another.

Mahatu was an adult female Sumatran rhino and had never before been with a male. Her reaction was not one of love at first sight. To understand what happened when the two

The outdoor rhino yard at the Cincinnati Zoo

rhinos first met, you need to know a little about how rhinos communicate with each other. They are naturally shy animals, and they will charge at just about anything that threatens them.

At first Mahatu, the female, was very territorial. Her actions said, "This is my space and what are you doing here? And more importantly, what are you doing eating my hay?" She bleeted out loud noises and spent a lot of time sniffing Bagus and nudging him with her horn. Eventually, Bagus seemed fed up and charged Mahatu, backing her up across the rhino yard. It was never really a fight, just two rhinos getting to know one another the way rhinos do.

Unfortunately, in the spring of 1992 Mahatu, the female rhino, died. The animal's liver—a vital body organ—was not functioning. The veterinarians believe this was a congenital, or inherited, problem and they could not save her. However, a great deal was learned from Mahatu. So little was known about Sumatran rhinos, that even after her death zoo veterinarians from around the country worked together to study her disease. The information they gain might help other rhinos in captivity remain healthy. The Cincinnati Zoo is waiting to receive another female rhino so that captive breeding efforts can be continued.

No Sumatran rhinos have been born in the United States yet. However, the Sumatran Rhino Trust hopes it will soon have four breeding pairs of rhinos in the breeding center in Indonesia, and another four pairs—one for each Trust zoo—in the United States.

Bagus at home in Cincinnati

A GLOBAL NETWORK

A cooperative network called the Species Survival Plan, or SSP, is in charge of the breeding of endangered species in American zoos. In this system, a team of scientists studies the captive animals to decide which ones should be bred with each other.

Right now, since all the Sumatran rhinos in our zoos have come from the wild, they are probably not closely related to each other. Each animal's genetic inheritance is different. But when the few captive animals are bred, and their young are born in zoos, scientists will need to manage the captive-breeding program carefully to guard against *inbreeding*—the mating of related animals. Inbreeding can produce offspring with a greater number of inherited disorders. Inbreeding rarely takes place in the wild, where there are more rhinos, but the zoos will need to work to mate animals with greater *biological*

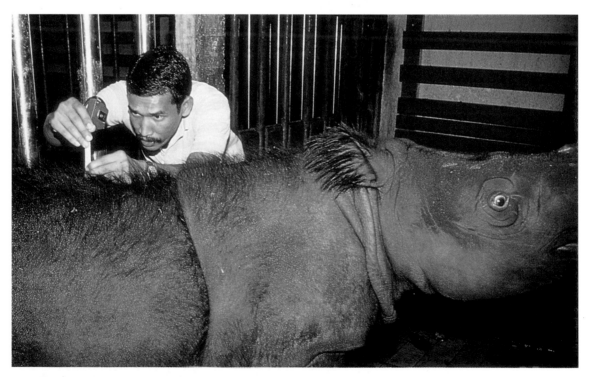

This Indonesian scientist is collecting hair samples to use to study the genetic diversity of Sumatran rhinos.

A century ago, thousands of Sumatran rhinos like Bagus roamed the rain forest. Today, only about 800 are left on Earth.

diversity, or differences. In order to do this, careful records will be needed and offspring will often be moved from one facility to another, including back to protected areas in Sumatra.

The long-term goal of the project is for Bagus's offspring to make a return trip and become stars of a story titled "A Rhino Goes Home to the Wild."

WHY SAVE RHINOS?

Rhino conservation aims to save more than just rhinos. The goal is to save the entire living *ecosystem* in which the rhinos live. In the case of the Sumatran rhino, that is the tropical rain forests of Indonesia. And saving the rain forest isn't about saving just

Tropical rain forests provide homes for orangutans and thousands of other wildlife species.

rhinos, parrots, and pythons. It is really about saving ourselves. By saving the Sumatran rhino habitat, we will be preserving the biological diversity of all the plants and animals that share their home.

THE FUTURE OF RHINOS

Rhinos are not disappearing because people do not like them. They are vanishing because there are too many people. In Indonesia, as nearly everywhere in the world today, there is a gigantic human population explosion. This means people are crowding out wild animals and the wild places where they live.

In 1650 there were around 500 million people on Earth. Two centuries later, in 1850, that number had grown to 1.2 billion. Just one century later, in 1950, the number of human beings more than doubled to 2.5 billion. And by 1987 it had doubled once again and there were 5 billion people on Earth. Scientists estimate that the human population will reach 11 billion by the year 2032. So it is easy to see that we are quickly running out of room on our planet.

In Indonesia and other areas with large populations, people often need the land that provides shelter for the forest animals.

The nation of Indonesia has the fourth largest population of any country on Earth, on a land mass only one-fifth the size of the United States. United Nations estimates show China with the largest human population: 1,130,065,000. India is second, with 844,000,000 people. Third is the United States, with 248,707,873 people, and fourth is Indonesia's 191,266,000 people.

CAN RHINOS BE SAVED?

Yes—the Sumatran rhinoceros is not doomed to extinction. But people need to learn to live successfully with nature in order to save space for rhinos. The steps that need to be taken to save the Sumatran rhino include:

Providing reasons for people to want to save the forests where the rhinos live. Local people need to be able to earn money through limited logging (along with replanting) and gathering of other forest products so that they do not clear all the trees. Like people everywhere, they must be able to feed their families before they can take care of nature.

Supporting research to learn more about the rhinos and their needs in the wild and their breeding cycle for successful reproduction in captivity.

Establishing and maintaining protected areas. Habitat is the most important factor in saving the Sumatran rhino. Protecting vital areas in a way that can be maintained over the long term is the most important of all conservation concerns.

Providing technical assistance. Throughout the developing world, committed conservationists are working against the tide in their native countries. Developed nations need to provide more assistance for wildlife conservation efforts instead of only promoting further development.

Coordinating captive breeding efforts around the world, in zoos and in the wild.

Enacting and enforcing conservation laws that would call for automatic jail sentences for poaching rhinos or destroying protected habitat. Funding is needed to provide guards to protect the rhinos.

Conservation education. All over the world people need to become better informed and more involved in wildlife conservation. The largest part of this task is insuring that wildlife and wild areas are protected not merely for their own sake, but also for the benefit of people living in and near those areas.

GLOSSARY

biological diversity—the natural variation of species that provides the genetic base for all life on Earth

captive breeding—propagation in captivity, often in an attempt to increase the population of a species critically low in number in the wild

deforestation—clear-cutting, or the clearing or alteration of forest habitat

ecosystem—a community of all living things together with its environment

endangered—a species reduced to the point of extinction, or nearly disappearing completely

habitat—the particular area and physical conditions where an animal or plant lives in the wild

habitat destruction—loss of an animal or plant species' native habitat due to human encroachment or natural causes, such as overdevelopment, logging, volcanic action, agriculture, or forest fires

inbreeding—the interbreeding of closely related animals, resulting in reduced genetic diversity

poaching—illegal hunting of a species

population—a group of the same species living in a given area

predator—an animal (or sometimes even a plant) that kills and eats other animals

range—the wild area in which a species is found

species—a specific kind of plant or animal that can mate and produce young like themselves

SUGGESTED READING

Bernard, Hans-Ulrich, Ed. *South East Asia Wildlife.* Singapore: APA Publications, 1991.

Huxley, Julian, Ed. *The Atlas of World Wildlife.* Portland House Publishing, 1973.

Lean, Geoffrey. *World Wildlife Fund Atlas of the Environment.* New York: Prentice Hall Press, 1990.

Macdonald, David, Ed. *The Encyclopedia of Mammals.* New York: Facts on File Publications, 1984.

Maynard, Thane. *Saving Endangered Mammals: A Field Guide to Some of the Earth's Rarest Animals.* New York: Franklin Watts, 1992.

Nowak, Ronald, Ed. *Walker's Guide to the Mammals.* Volume II, Fifth Edition. Baltimore: The Johns Hopkins University Press, 1991.

Oey, Edward, Ed. *Indonesia.* Singapore: APA Publications, 1989.

ZOOBOOKS. *Rhinos.* 930 W. Washington Street, San Diego, CA, 92103.

BIBLIOGRAPHY

Bernard, Hans-Ulrich, Ed. *South East Asia Wildlife*. Singapore: APA Publications, 1991.

Foose, Thomas and Zainuddin, Zainal Zahari. *International Studbook for Sumatran Rhino*. Bethesda, Maryland: American Association of Zoological Parks and Aquariums, 1991.

Lean, Geoffrey. *World Wildlife Fund Atlas of the Environment*. New York: Prentice Hall Press, 1990.

Oey, Edward, Ed. *Indonesia*. Singapore: APA Publications, 1989.

Van Strien, Nico. *The Sumatran Rhinoceros in the Gunung Leuser National Park, Sumatra, Indonesia; Its Distribution, Ecology and Conservation*. Hamburg and Berlin: Verlag Paul Parey Publishers, 1986.

Widada, Ir., Ed. *Sumatran Rhino Captive Breeding Programme*. Bogor, West Java: Indonesian Center for Reproduction of Endangered Wildlife, 1991.

ZOOBOOKS. *Rhinos*. 930 W. Washington Street, San Diego, CA, 92103.

INDEX

ASIA

1900
THE HISTORIC RANGE
OF THE SUMATRAN
RHINOCEROS

SOUTHEAST ASIA

PACIFIC OCEAN

MALAYSIA

SUMATRA

INDIAN OCEAN

BORNEO

INDONESIA

JAVA

ASIA

SOUTHEAST ASIA

PACIFIC OCEAN

MALAYSIA

SUMATRA

INDIAN OCEAN

BORNEO

INDONESIA

JAVA

Bagus's Journey

Amsterdam

Cincinnati

Los Angeles

Sumatra